Decodable Stories
Takehome Books

Grade 2

Joshua Chang

4

McGraw Hill Education

Bothell, WA • Chicago, IL • Columbus, OH • New York, NY

Contents

About the Decodable Stories Takehome Books

The **SRA Open Court Reading** *Decodable Stories Takehome Books* allow your students to apply their knowledge of phonic elements to read simple, engaging texts. Each story supports instruction in a new phonic element and incorporates elements and words that have been learned earlier.

The students can fold and staple the pages of each *Decodable Story Takehome Book* to make books of their own to keep and read. We suggest that you keep extra sets of the stories in your classroom for the children to reread.

How to Make a Takehome Book

1. Tear out the pages you need.

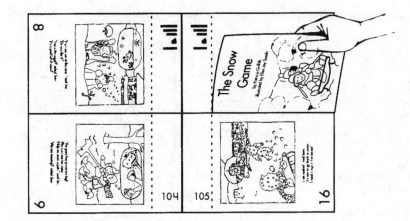

2. Place the title page facedown and the page with two consecutive folios (pages 4–5 in example) faceup.

For 16-page book

3. Place the pages on top of each other in order. The facedown title page will be on the bottom, and the page with the consecutive folios (pages 8–9 in example) will be faceup on the top.

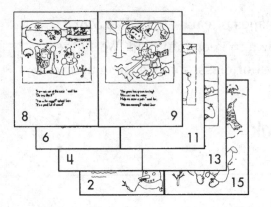

4. Fold along the center line.

5. Check to make sure the pages are in order.

6. Staple the pages along the fold.

For 8-page book

3. Place the page with consecutive folios (page 4–5 in example) on top of the other page.

4. Fold along the center line.

5. Check to make sure the pages are in order.

6. Staple the pages along the fold.

Just to let you know...

A message from _____

Help your child discover the joy of independent reading with *SRA Open Court Reading*. From time to time your child will bring home his or her very own *Decodable Stories Takehome Books* to share with you. With your help, these stories can give your child important reading practice and a joyful shared reading experience.

You may want to set aside a few minutes every evening to read these stories together. Here are some suggestions you may find helpful:

- Do not expect your child to read each story perfectly, but concentrate on sharing the book together.
- Participate by doing some of the reading.
- Talk about the stories as you read, give lots of encouragement, and watch as your child becomes more fluent throughout the year!

Learning to read takes lots of practice. Sharing these stories is one way that your child can gain that valuable practice. Encourage your child to keep the *Decodable Stories Takehome Books* in a special place. This collection will make a library of books that your child can read and reread. Take the time to listen to your child read from his or her library. Just a few moments of shared reading each day can give your child the confidence needed to excel in reading.

Children who read every day come to think of reading as a pleasant, natural part of life. One way to inspire your child to read is to show that reading is an important part of your life by letting him or her see you reading books, magazines, newspapers, or any other materials. Another good way to show that you value reading is to share a *Decodable Story Takehome Book* with your child each day.

Successful reading experiences allow children to be proud of their new-found reading ability. Support your child with interest and enthusiasm about reading. You won't regret it!

MHEonline.com

Send all inquiries to:
McGraw-Hill Education
8787 Orion Place
Columbus, OH 43240

Sand, Tan Hats, and a Mat

by Diane Webber
illustrated by Judy Nostrandt

Decodable Story 1

Bothell, WA • Chicago, IL • Columbus, OH • New York, NY

Matt, Sam, and Dan sat.
Matt, Sam, and Dan sat at Matt's.

Dan, Sam, and Dad stand and give Matt a hand.

"May I?" said Matt.
"Take these tan hats, sand, and mat," said Dad.

"I am Matt's dad. May I help?"

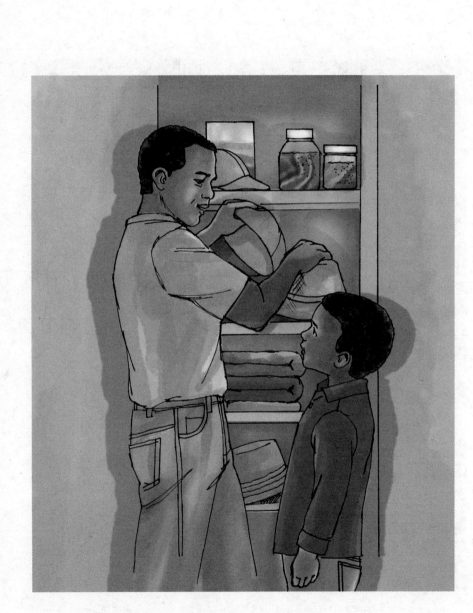

Dad had sand, tan hats, and a mat.
"Matt, stand and give me a hand with these hats."

"Look!" said Sam.
Matt and Dan stand.

MHEonline.com

Send all inquiries to:
McGraw-Hill Education
8787 Orion Place
Columbus, OH 43240

Hats!

by Tamera Stanley
illustrated by Chris Vallo

Decodable Story 2

Bothell, WA • Chicago, IL • Columbus, OH • New York, NY

Dad and Nan had hats.
Dad and Nan had a hat stand.

Stan has a yellow hat.
Sam has a tan hat.

"May sad Stan have a yellow hat?" said Nan.
"And may sad Sam have a tan hat?" said Nan.

"Nan, give Dan and Stan these hats," said Dad.

"And give Sam and Tam these hats."

Stan and Dan had tan hats.
Sam and Tam had yellow hats.

MHEonline.com

Send all inquiries to:
McGraw-Hill Education
8787 Orion Place
Columbus, OH 43240

Cass, Bill, and Mitt

by Cassandra Miller
illustrated by Marilyn Janovitz

Decodable Story 3

Bothell, WA • Chicago, IL • Columbus, OH • New York, NY

These mints are for Bill and Mitt.
If Bill can stand, Cass may give him mints.

Cass can hand Bill and Mitt no mints.
These mints are for Cass.

A cat hid. Bill, Mitt, and a cat go!

Bill did stand! Cass can hand him mints.

If Mitt can jump, Cass may give him mints.
Mitt did it! Cass can hand him mints.

Can Bill and Mitt sit?
Can Cass hand Bill and Mitt mints?

MHEonline.com

Send all inquiries to:
McGraw-Hill Education
8787 Orion Place
Columbus, OH 43240

Mitts and Hits

by Daniel Wells
illustrated by Anna Cota Robles

Decodable Story 4

Bothell, WA • Chicago, IL • Columbus, OH • New York, NY

Kim and Bill had been to the Sand Pit before.

26

22

Bill and Kim had been to the Sand Pit!

31

Kim and Bill did hit!
Kim hits. Bam! Bill claps.
Bill hits. Bap! Kim claps.

Bill and Kim stand on a ramp.
Kim had a mitt, and Bill had a mitt.
"Those are our mitts."

Bill had a bat. Kim had a bat.
"Those are our bats."

28

Did Kim hit? Did Bill hit?
Did Kim miss? Did Bill miss?

29

MHEonline.com

Send all inquiries to:
McGraw-Hill Education
8787 Orion Place
Columbus, OH 43240

A Big Fan

by Cassandra Miller
illustrated by Audrey Durney

Decodable Story 5

Bothell, WA • Chicago, IL • Columbus, OH • New York, NY

Mom and Fran had gifts for Gramps.
"Mom, I am hot! Our big dog Kip is hot."

Kip likes a big fan.

Did Kip spot Mom flip the fan off?
If Mom can flip it, can Kip?

Mom got a big fan. Fran saw Mom flip it on.
Did Kip spot Mom flip it on, too?

Mom and Fran like a big fan.
Kip likes a big fan.

"We can drop off those gifts," said Mom.
Mom had to flip the fan off.

MHEonline.com

Send all inquiries to:
McGraw-Hill Education
8787 Orion Place
Columbus, OH 43240

A Best Pig Pin

by Jeffrey Allen
illustrated by Paul Meisel

Decodable Story 6

Bothell, WA • Chicago, IL • Columbus, OH • New York, NY

Jeff sat in a tent. A man on a box read, "Mrs. Peg Webb will win for best ox."

Jeff read the pin and got a big grin. Max was the best pig and the best pet!

The man read, "Mr. Jeff West will win for best pig!"
"Jeff, you win!" said Dad.

Jeff felt glad. Mrs. Webb did a lot to help Max,
Jeff's pet pig.

"Mr. Ben Grant will win for best jam." Dad and Jeff clap.

Next came the best pet pig pin. Jeff felt hot!

MHEonline.com

Copyright © 2015 McGraw-Hill Education

Send all inquiries to:
McGraw-Hill Education
8787 Orion Place
Columbus, OH 43240

A Contest

by Giulia Verzariu
illustrated by Rachel Ivanyi

Decodable Story 7

Bothell, WA • Chicago, IL • Columbus, OH • New York, NY

Max is a frog. Max hops off a big log.
Next, Max hops off boxes.

"Let's stop to have bread and jam," said Max.
Jeff said, "A rest is good for me!"

Max heads fast past a big log.
Jeff hops past a log and Max!

Max hops past plants. Max hops fast for bread and jam. Max did not stop!

"I hop fast. I am the best. Tell me, who can hop fast?" asks Max.

"I hop fast," Jeff said.
"Let's have a contest to tell who is best," said Max.

MHEonline.com

Copyright © 2015 McGraw-Hill Education

Send all inquiries to:
McGraw-Hill Education
8787 Orion Place
Columbus, OH 43240

Gwen Must Run

by Luke Fisher
illustrated by Karen Tafoya

Decodable Story 8

Bothell, WA • Chicago, IL • Columbus, OH • New York, NY

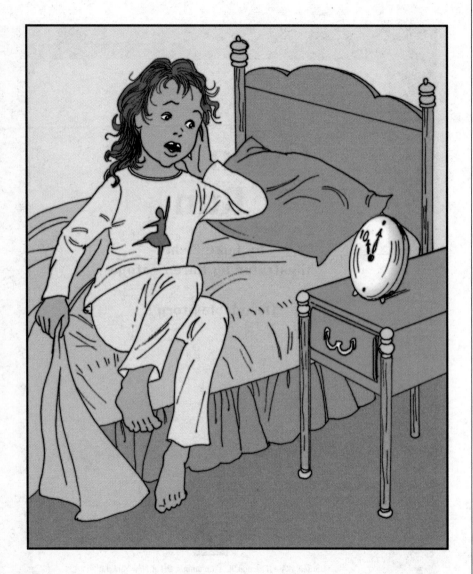

Gwen gets up at ten.
"I had to miss the bus!" she yells.

"There is no class," Mr. Buzz tells Gwen.
Gwen tells Mr. Buzz, "Then I did not miss the bus!"

"Can I help?" Mr. Buzz asks.
Gwen tells Mr. Buzz, "It's past ten, but I cannot get in!"

Gwen runs past her mom.
Gwen tells her mom, "I must run!"

Gwen zigzags past her pal Val.
"Will you jump with us?" asks Val.
"I must run!" yells Gwen.

"Will you stop and visit us?" Mrs. Yip asks.
"I must run!" Gwen tells her. "I cannot quit!"

MHEonline.com

Copyright © 2015 McGraw-Hill Education

Send all inquiries to:
McGraw-Hill Education
8787 Orion Place
Columbus, OH 43240

Buzz, Buzz, Buzz

by Valerie Glickman
illustrated by Merrill Rainey

Decodable Story 9

Bothell, WA • Chicago, IL • Columbus, OH • New York, NY

Quinn slept. Buzz! Buzz! Buzz!
That buzz meant Quinn had to get up. But Quinn did
not. Quinn felt he still must rest.

"Bam, bam, bam will get a red lump up!" she said.

Mom got Quinn's drum. Mom hit it fast. Bam! Bam! Bam! Mom saw Quinn jump!

As Mom came up the steps, Quinn hid his head. When Mom saw Quinn in bed, she had to grin.

"Quinn, you are just a red lump!" Mom said.
Mom did not see Quinn grin, too.

"Buzz, buzz, buzz did not get a red lump up," said Mom.
Quinn still hid.

MHEonline.com

Send all inquiries to:
McGraw-Hill Education
8787 Orion Place
Columbus, OH 43240

Chips

by Chester Shipley
illustrated by C. A. Nobens

Decodable Story 10

Bothell, WA • Chicago, IL • Columbus, OH • New York, NY

Upon a shelf sits a dish of chips. Seth is a big chips fan. Is that shelf too far up?

Crash! The dish and chips hit Seth! But Seth is glad. He grabs chips to munch!

"I wish I could get chips! I will jump!" yells Seth. Then Seth did jump. Crash! Seth hit the shelf!

6

Seth sets a box upon a bench. Could that box get Seth far up?

3

Seth is still an inch away! Seth sets a thin rug upon the box.

With the thin rug, Seth can just brush his hand on the dish. Seth still cannot get that dish.

MHEonline.com

Send all inquiries to:
McGraw-Hill Education
8787 Orion Place
Columbus, OH 43240

The Red Star

by Lynn Frankel
illustrated by Judy Nostrandt

Decodable Story 11

Bothell, WA • Chicago, IL • Columbus, OH • New York, NY

Mark, Chad, and Trish sit in a park. Mark calls out, "This is not much fun in the dark."

Mark kids Chad, "I wish you were smart."
Chad yells, "I am smart!"
Mark grins, "But you just wished upon Mars, not a star!"

"For which do you wish?" Chad asks Mark.
"Cash? Cars?"

"Let's wish upon a star!" Chad grins.
"Which star?" asks Trish.
"Start with that red star!" yells Chad.

"I will start," calls Chad. "I wish to be rich. I want as much cash as I can get!"

Then Trish is next. "I want a fast car. When I want to, I can zip to far off lands!"

12

13

MHEonline.com

Send all inquiries to:
McGraw-Hill Education
8787 Orion Place
Columbus, OH 43240

A Bridge

**by Gretchen Decker
illustrated by Paul Meisel**

Decodable Story 12

Bothell, WA • Chicago, IL • Columbus, OH • New York, NY

This bridge is big! Jack's class will walk over it and back.

That big ship will go to a dock. Jack would like to visit that dock!

But that ship can fit under the bridge. How can they pack such big stacks on it?

Cars and trucks go past. Jack never looks at traffic. Jack looks at this big bridge! Jack spots a patch of mist.

Jack stands at the bridge's edge. Jack can see dark water in spots.

20

Then Jack spots a big ship. Can it pass under this bridge? It will never fit. Will it hit this bridge? It will scratch it!

21

MHEonline.com

Send all inquiries to:
McGraw-Hill Education
8787 Orion Place
Columbus, OH 43240

A Lunch List

by Dennis Fertig
illustrated by Merrill Rainey

Decodable Story 13

Bothell, WA • Chicago, IL • Columbus, OH • New York, NY

Jess had to get eight lunches for eight pals. Plus Jess had to get lunch, too. Jess had to get nine lunches.

26

As Jess jogged to a lunch truck, Mack spotted Jess's list on his desk. Mack grinned. "Jess will get back very fast," Mack said.

Jess slipped on dark sunglasses. "I will fetch luch and be back fast," Jess yelled to Mack.

Jess grabbed a pen and printed a list. Eight lunches had to have sandwiches. Jess's lunch had to have a sandwich.

Jess had to get nine cups for water. Jess had to get napkins and dishes.

Jess checked her list. Jess asked Mack to check it. Mack said, "This list is good!"

MHEonline.com

Send all inquiries to:
McGraw-Hill Education
8787 Orion Place
Columbus, OH 43240

No Drinks
in Class

by Luke Fisher
illustrated by John Edwards

Decodable Story 14

Bothell, WA • Chicago, IL • Columbus, OH • New York, NY

It is the end of May. Our class is hot. It is hard to think.

When the bell rings, I start singing. Thank you bell! Thanks, Mrs. Bridges!

I am stuck in this hot class. I am sweating and sticking to my desk. "This stinks!" I think.

Bring me a bucket of water. I will splash and have fun.

Pick a dock, and I will jump off it. I will not sink.

If I were king, I'd sing, "Bring things to drink. Bring six pink drinks!"

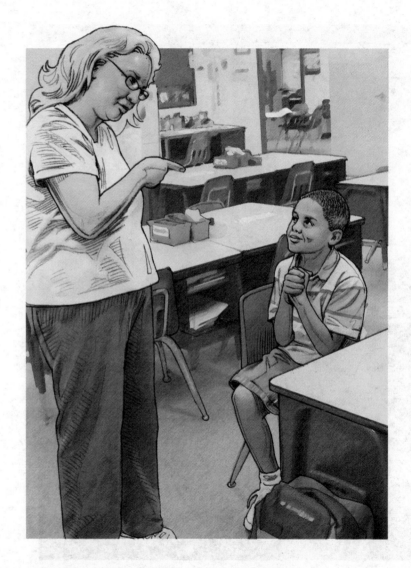

I beg, but Mrs. Bridges will not budge.
She tells me, "No drinks in class!"

MHEonline.com

Send all inquiries to:
McGraw-Hill Education
8787 Orion Place
Columbus, OH 43240

Paddle, Duck, Paddle

by Eileen Breeze
illustrated by Stephanie Pershing

Decodable Story 15

Bothell, WA • Chicago, IL • Columbus, OH • New York, NY

Hank is a little duck. He zings past a puddle and gravel.
"I will get a snack," Hank thinks.

The girl fumbles and tosses bread to Hank. Hank gobbles it up and quacks, "Thank you!"

Hank quacks, flapping his wings.
"Look, a little duck!" giggles one of the seven.
"I think little ducks like to gobble bread!"

46

"I want bread. That's why I will use my head to get bread!"

43

Hank paddles to the middle of the pond and spots seven girls picnicking on the bank.

"Why, I think they will have bread!"

"I must use these strong legs to paddle!" Hank puffs. "I'm traveling as fast as I can."

44

45

MHEonline.com

Send all inquiries to:
McGraw-Hill Education
8787 Orion Place
Columbus, OH 43240

Learning to Swim

by Eileen Breeze
illustrated by John Edwards

Decodable Story 16

Bothell, WA • Chicago, IL • Columbus, OH • New York, NY

"When can I learn to swim, Dad?" asks Burt.
"Let's start after lunch," Dad tells Burt.

"Dad, I have never had this much fun!" yells
Burt. "And I can still learn to swim much better!"

First, Burt stands up. Then Burt jumps!
Burt's head is under the water!

After lunch, Dad helps Burt learn to swim.
"Dad, will I get hurt in the water?"
"I will never let you get hurt, Burt."

First, Burt puts his legs under the water.
Then his arms are under the water!

Burt is swimming a little better.
"Dad, may I jump in the water?" Burt asks.
"Yes!" grins Dad.

MHEonline.com

Send all inquiries to:
McGraw-Hill Education
8787 Orion Place
Columbus, OH 43240

Farm Chores

by Edward Bricker
illustrated by Karen Tafoya

Decodable Story 17

Bothell, WA • Chicago, IL • Columbus, OH • New York, NY

Dora is a farmer. In the morning she gets up in the dark to do her chores.

Dora grins. Here is the sun!
"I wish one more thing. I wish all days were just like this!"

Dora sits on her horse. "Run fast!" The horse jumps. "Faster! Faster!" Dora yells. "We must be quick or we will miss the sun getting up!"

"I wish I did not have chores," she thinks. "But I like to be with the animals."

"I wish upon that star!" Dora thinks, "No chores!"

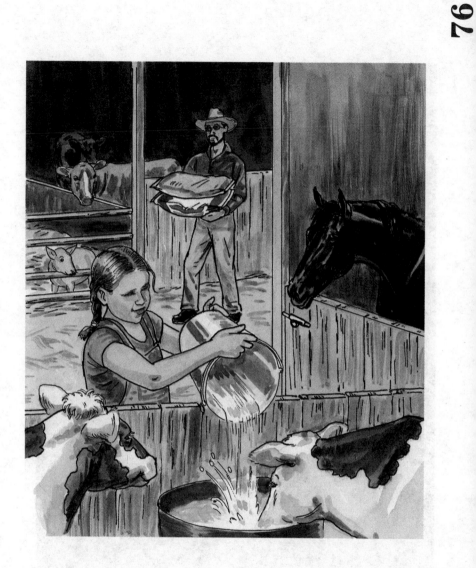

Dora brings water for the animals.
"I still have more chores!" Dora mutters. "I must ride the black horse to the store."

MHEonline.com

Send all inquiries to:
McGraw-Hill Education
8787 Orion Place
Columbus, OH 43240

Tracks at a Pond

by Valerie Glickman
illustrated by Chris Vallo

Decodable Story 18

Bothell, WA • Chicago, IL • Columbus, OH • New York, NY

Did you spot tracks in dirt at a pond? Which animal left them? That can be a puzzle at first.

Ducks paddle in ponds. Did you spot a duck's tracks? Kids walk at ponds. Did you spot more tracks?

Chipmunks run past ponds. Chipmunks live in long dirt tunnels. Bobcats can catch chipmunks. Did you spot chipmunk tracks?

Turtles live at ponds. Did you spot turtle tracks in that dirt?

On a pond's edge, birds and skunks look for turtle eggs. Did you spot bird or skunk tracks by eggshells?

A bobcat hunts after dark. Bobcat tracks can be hard to spot. Did you spot bobcat tracks?

Kate's Picnic

by Sean Saunders
illustrated by Barbara Counseller

Decodable Story 19

Bothell, WA • Chicago, IL • Columbus, OH • New York, NY

Kate and her pals are planning a picnic. The picnic will be in Kate's backyard. Jane and Jan will come.

2

Kate helped Dad take in things from the yard.
"You did a caring thing for your brother," Dad said.
"He's just a little kid," said Kate.

After a game, Jan and Jane had to go. Kate and Damon waved. Jan and Jane did the same.

Kate made sandwiches. Her mom baked cornbread. Jan will bring apples. Jane made punch to drink.

Kate set plates on the table in the shade. Then Jane and Jan came!

4

"Yes!" said Damon. "I am Picnic Man! I make the picnic safe!"
Damon and the girls had fun.

Mom came and cut the cornbread.

"Damon, did Kate ask you to her picnic?" Mom asked. She gave Kate a wink.

Kate's little brother Damon came, too. Damon had on his cape and his acorn cap.

"No, Damon!" yelled Kate. "This picnic is for girls!"

"I am Picnic Man!" said Damon. "I will make the picnic safe! I want apples! I want sandwiches!"

6

"Take a sandwich, Damon," said Kate.
"Take an apple," said Jan.
Damon ate and drank a cup of punch.

"I can?" asked Damon. "Thanks!"
Damon gave the girls a big grin. He ran back to the picnic.

"Damon, you are just a little kid," said Kate. "You can't come to this picnic."

Damon felt sad.

"I never get to have fun with Kate," he said. And then he went away.

8

Jan whispered to Jane. Jane whispered to Kate. "Come back, Damon!" Jan said. "You can come to the picnic!"

9

89

Five Gifts for Mike

by Elizabeth Ramsey
illustrated by Anna Cota-Robles

Decodable Story 20

Bothell, WA • Chicago, IL • Columbus, OH • New York, NY

Mike and Kim like to ride bikes. They ride to the park, and Gran rides along.

Kim gives Mike the box of gifts. Gran hands him the card.

"You gave me the park!" Mike grins.

"Mind if I make a card for Mike?" asks Gran. "He likes catfish. I will give him one."
Kim hides Mike's gifts in a tin box.

Mike, Kim, and Gran lock the bikes. They like to hike to the pond.

They hike in a line. They hike for a mile. Gran is first and then Kim and then Mike.

Kim and Gran take the gifts to Mike. But first, Gran must make a quick stop.

Then Kim finds a big white feather. She gathers a nut, and she picks up a dime. Kim has five gifts that Mike will like.

Five white ducks swim in the pond. The ducks quack and dive. They nibble insects.

Fins make ripples on the pond.
"What kinds of fish swim in the pond?" asks Mike.

Next Kim finds a little tan shell. These are things that will make Mike smile.

Kim thinks of gifts that Mike will like. She picks up a rock that shines in the sun.

Gran tells Mike, "That kind is a sunfish, and the black fish is a catfish."

"I like the catfish best!" yells Mike.

The fish swam and hid under a rock.

The next time they ride, it is just Kim and Gran. Mike is sick. He must rest in bed.

Kim tells Gran that she misses Mike.
"We can find a gift for Mike," Gran tells Kim.
"Yes!" smiles Kim. "I will find him one!"

MHEonline.com

Send all inquiries to:
McGraw-Hill Education
8787 Orion Place
Columbus, OH 43240

The Mole Zone

by Sean Saunders
illustrated by Stephanie Pershing

Decodable Story 21

Bothell, WA • Chicago, IL • Columbus, OH • New York, NY

It is a fine morning. The sun is shining. The birds are singing. Dad is going to get the paper.

"The mole *is* little and helpless," Mom admits. "We can have a mole zone, can't we?"

"Hold on," Cole chimes in. "The mole broke just two little buds. Old Buster digs holes for his bones, but you don't give him a cold squirt!"

"This is the best yard on the block," Dad thinks. "The grass is perfect, and the garden is lush."

That is when Dad spots the hole. Next to the hole is a dome of dirt.

"No, no," he mutters, "not a mole!"

Mom tells Cole, "Hold this cup while I get the hose! I'll give that mole a cold, wet squirt!"

Mom, in her robe, runs to the open gate.
"Don't let that mole rob my roses," she yells.

"A mole will not stop at a single hole. This mole must go, and it must go now."

"Mr. Mole, you have got to go now!" Dad yells.
But Mr. Mole is not at home.

"No, no! You two are both no help! You are supposed to chase that mole!" scolds Dad as he opens the gate. The mole gets an insect off a rosebud.

Both Bandit and Buster like this thing. Bandit gives it a lick. Old Buster and the mole are nose to nose.

The mole is rolling over the grass. It is headed for the garden!

The mole heads under the gate. Over the hedge jumps
Bandit the cat.
"Go, Bandit, Go!" yells Dad. "Get that mole!"

At that, Old Buster the dog wakes up.
"Bark at that mole, Buster!! Send him packing!"
Old Buster trots over and sniffs the mole.

MHEonline.com

Send all inquiries to:
McGraw-Hill Education
8787 Orion Place
Columbus, OH 43240

Hope's Cute Music Box

by Margaret Mason
illustrated by Judy Nostrandt

Decodable Story 22

Bothell, WA • Chicago, IL • Columbus, OH • New York, NY

This is Hope. She is the best artist in her class. She uses lots of art things in her projects.

50

Hope shares the art things in her music box. "We can all make better art if we share!"

63

Hope yells at her sister, "Use the music box, fine! Just ask first next time!"

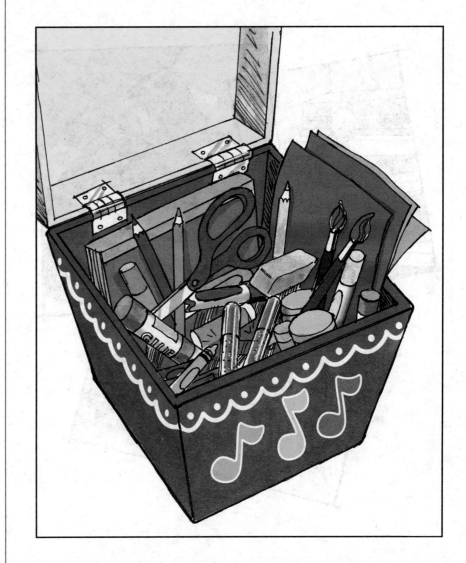

Hope has the cutest cube-shaped music box. She stores her art things in it. But Hope has lost her music box.

Hope goes looking for her music box. She finds her lost mule and a human model. Hope cannot find her cute music box.

But Hope is in for a surprise. Her cute cube-shaped box sits on her bed. A note from her sister is on it.

Later, Hope walks home thinking. She will have to buy art things. She cannot afford to buy a cute music box for a while.

It is time for art class. There is zero time to buy art things. With zero art things, Hope thinks it is useless to go to class.

Hope goes to art class and sits at the table.
"You don't have your cute box?" asks Robin.
"Use this paper."
"Thanks!"

The art class starts. Even with no cute music box,
Hope makes art. Hope uses her pals' art things.

Simone asks the class, "Can we gather all the pastels?"
The class yells, "Yes! Then we can all use them."

"Use this, too," adds Will. "I can tell you like red."
Hope tells Will, "Thanks! This will be useful."

Justin lets Hope use his markers. He shares his music, as well. Hope likes to make art with music.

Stella sits across from Hope. She hands over glitter and paste.

"You can use this glitter and paste," Stella tells Hope.

MHEonline.com

Send all inquiries to:
McGraw-Hill Education
8787 Orion Place
Columbus, OH 43240

A Good Life at the Lake

by Grace Trubiano
illustrated by Stephanie Pershing

Decodable Story 23

Bothell, WA • Chicago, IL • Columbus, OH • New York, NY

"Rise and shine, Kate!" said Mom. "It is another fine morning! Let's go to the lake and hike."

66

"Kate!" said Mom.
"Just kidding!" grinned Kate as the fish swam away.
Kate and Mom had a good time at the lake.

"May I take it home with us?" asked Kate. "It will be mine! I will name it Goldfish."

So Kate and her mom went to the lake for a hike. They spotted many plants and animals.

"Look at this, Mom!" said Kate.
"Did you find an animal?" asked Mom.
"I see the cutest little frog!" said Kate.

"Look, Mom!" said Kate.
"Look where? Did you find a bigger animal?" asked Mom.
"I just spotted a cute fish!" said Kate.

Mom gave Kate a big hug.

"Let's wade in the lake now," said Mom. "Perhaps you can see another animal."

"Can I take it home with us?" asked Kate. "It will be mine. I will name it Spike!"

Just then, the frog ate a bug. And it ate another bug. "Can you find lots of bugs?" asked Mom.

"The frog has a good life at the lake," said Kate. "I don't think it's wise to take the frog home with us."

"Not so fine, I suppose," said Kate.
The frog hopped away. Kate gave a sad little wave.
"Where did the frog go?" asked Mom.

"Yes," smiled Kate. "I can find many bugs at home in the backyard."
Kate kept smiling at her mom.

"How will this frog survive at home?" asked Mom.
"I can use a box to make the safest home ever," said Kate.

"Hold on!" said Mom. "Now the frog has a big lake.
Compared to a lake, how is a little box better as a home?"

MHEonline.com

Send all inquiries to:
McGraw-Hill Education
8787 Orion Place
Columbus, OH 43240

Uncle Jack

by Michael Knightly
illustrated by Paul Meisel

Decodable Story 24

Bothell, WA • Chicago, IL • Columbus, OH • New York, NY

Dad and I hid in long grass. Uncle Jack knelt next to us.
We hoped to spot a bird.

82

When Uncle Jack wrote, he wrote about Dad and me too.
And he wrote about Dad's joke!

95

The next day, that camera got sedge wren snapshots! "These snapshots are wonderful! I will start to write," said Uncle Jack.

Uncle Jack is a bird expert. He takes snapshots of birds. He writes about birds.

The bird we hoped to spot was a sedge wren. There are many kinds of wrens. Most are not hard to find. But the sedge wren is.

"I designed this camera. If a bird gets close, the camera takes snapshots," said Uncle Jack.

Uncle Jack had a camera in his knapsack. He set that camera on a branch. He used a wire knot so his camera would not get knocked down.

Most wrens have striped heads, but not the sedge wren. And it will not sing the same way as most wrens.

I saw a bird. "Is that it?" I asked.
"That is a wren, but the wrong kind," Uncle Jack said.

86

We still did not find a sedge wren! Is this the wrong
spot? Were the signs for the wrong bird?
"I have a plan to get snapshots," Uncle Jack told us.

91

The next day, we were back at that same spot. Would we see a sedge wren? We could not chat much. Dad could not make jokes.

At dark, we had to go. Uncle Jack said, "I see more than one sign that sedge wrens are close."

At his car, Uncle Jack told me a wren fact. "Did you
know that wrens dine on insects like gnats?"

"I dine on gnats when I ride my bike fast and sing,"
joked Dad.

Uncle Jack and I grinned.

MHEonline.com

Send all inquiries to:
McGraw-Hill Education
8787 Orion Place
Columbus, OH 43240

Edith and Pete

by Susan Martina
illustrated by Brenda Johnson

Decodable Story 25

Bothell, WA • Chicago, IL • Columbus, OH • New York, NY

Edith was taking a stroll along the river bank when she slipped into the river! The water in the river was fast!

An unplanned kindness does matter. We can all be like Edith and Pete!

Did you think Edith would be able to help Pete? What does this tell us? What can we learn from Edith and Pete?

Edith could not compete with the fast water. If she went under, then she would not make it.

Pete saw Edith struggling. Pete was a kind bird. He wanted to help. "She is not going to make it!" Pete said.

Because of these acts, Edith and Pete are both fine. If just one had not helped, this would not be.

Think about the kind acts that Edith and Pete did. Pete helped Edith, and Edith helped Pete.

"I will help that ant," Pete said. Pete got a blade of grass. He bent it down to the river.

"Here!" Pete yelled, "Grab this blade of grass!" Edith got out of the river. Edith was safe.

The cat yelled, alerting Pete to get away. Now two kind acts were complete. Edith had returned Pete's kindness.

The cat crept up a little bit more. Edith reacted fast. Edith bit the cat before Pete even spotted it.

Pete went over next to Edith. "Are you hurt or sick?" asked Pete. "Do you have a fever?"

"No, I am fine," panted Edith. "Thanks. Because you helped me, I will help you in time."

Later, Edith saw a cat staring at Pete. "This cannot be good for Pete," Edith said. Edith had to help so Pete would be safe.

MHEonline.com

Send all inquiries to:
McGraw-Hill Education
8787 Orion Place
Columbus, OH 43240

Amazing Animals

by Dennis Fertig
illustrated by Marilyn Janovitz

Decodable Story 26

Bothell, WA • Chicago, IL • Columbus, OH • New York, NY

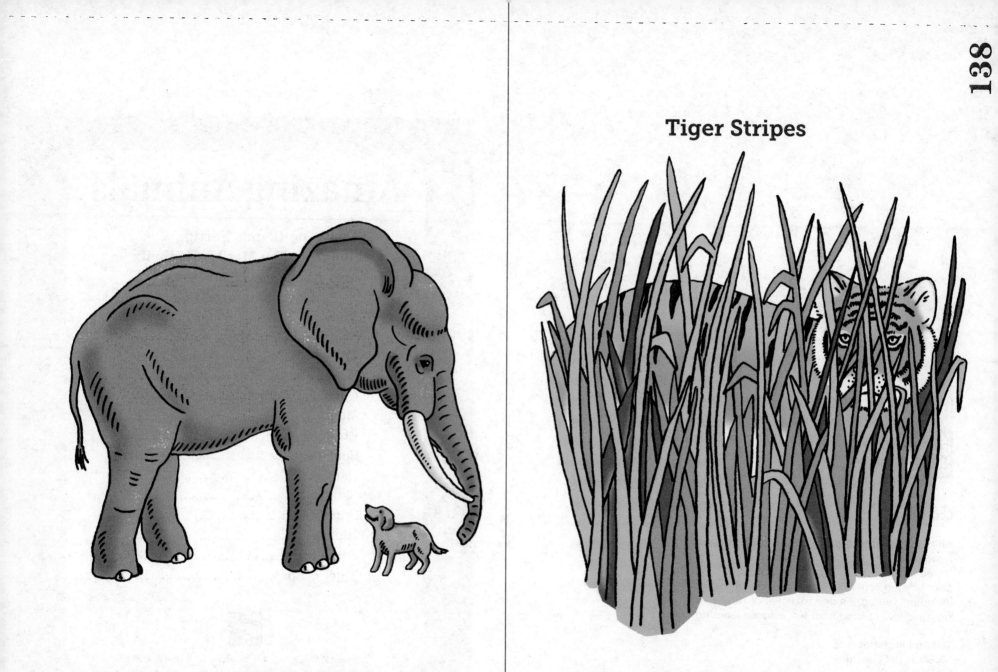

Tiger Stripes

Animals are amazing. Some are cute. Some are odd. Here are some fun animal facts.

A tiger's stripes help it hide in grass. That helps it hunt. Under its fur, a tiger's skin is still striped!

Zebra Stripes

Smart Pigs

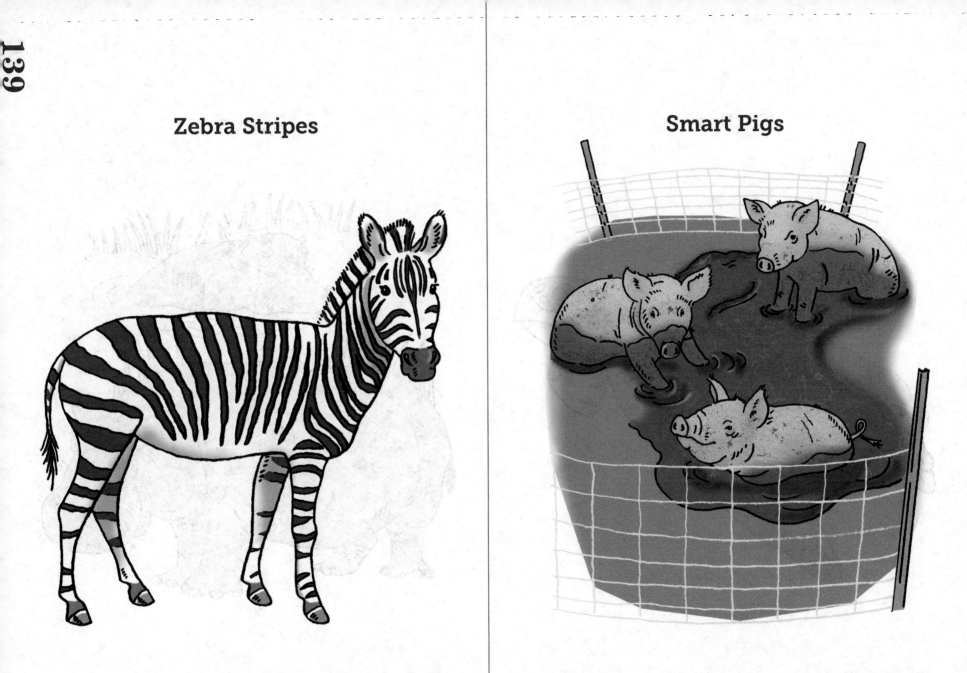

A zebra's stripes may help it hide. Its stripes may even save it from bug bites. Under its fur, a zebra's skin is black.

Pigs are smarter than most other animals. Pigs are even smarter than dogs. But chimps may be the smartest animals.

Turtles

Hippos

Turtle shells are made of bones. Those shells help some kinds of turtles live longer than humans.

Hippos have short, thick legs. Yet hippos can run fast. Hippos can even run faster than humans!

Stink Bugs

Whale Songs

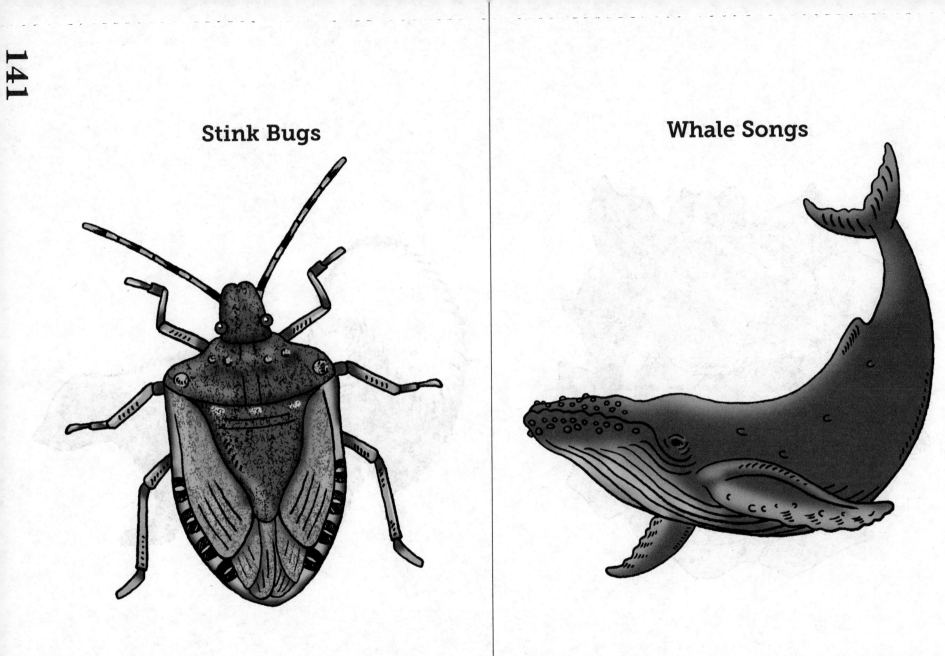

Stink bugs smell and taste bad. What would bite a stink bug? Other stink bugs! They don't mind the taste.

Whales sing! Whales sing to other whales. Whale songs may travel miles and miles under the water.

Cute Chipmunks

Skunks

Chipmunk homes have two parts. One part is a nest where chipmunks rest. Chipmunks use the other part to store nuts.

What animal would grab a skunk? A fox often will if it has no other snacks. Plus some birds like skunk dinners.

Bats

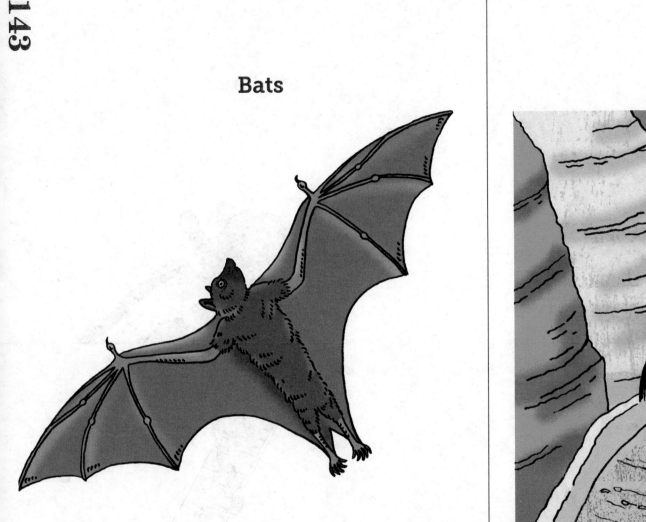

Bats can be rather big! One kind can open its wings as wide as humans can spread their arms.

Mules

A mule is a bit like a horse. Both can be the same size. If you ride on cliff paths, a mule is safer.

Bobcats

Spiders

Bobcats are two times as big as pet cats. Wild bobcats often live close to our homes! Yet we do not spot them.

Yikes! The biggest spider is the size of a dinner plate! It can catch little birds!

MHEonline.com

Send all inquiries to:
McGraw-Hill Education
8787 Orion Place
Columbus, OH 43240

A Good Deed at the Beach

by Marie Randolph
illustrated by Barbara Counseller

Decodable Story 27

Bothell, WA • Chicago, IL • Columbus, OH • New York, NY

Mom woke us up. "No more sleeping!" she said.
"We are going to the beach."
"Sweet!" we said.

We did not swim in the water, but we still had fun. And we did a good deed for the beach!

"Thanks for your help," the man said. "Here's a treat to eat."

He gave us a sheet to read. "If you are free, come back in three weeks!"

"Have a bite to eat," Mom said. "Then put on jeans and sneakers. No swim things this week."

"What do you mean?" we asked.
"Come and you will see," said Mom.
We got in the car and headed to the beach.

My sister said, "Now the beach is clean! I hope we can keep it neat and clean."

It did not seem to take long. We put all the bags in a big heap. Then we had a seat on the beach.

I could smell the sea. I could feel the breeze. I like to be on the beach.

Then Mom said, "Read that."

A poster read, "Clean up your beach. Please help!"
"We need to help," my sister said. I agreed.

My sister picked up a string of beads. I picked up a banana peel.
"At least I have these," I said.

"Sweep the beach!" the man said.

We picked up bags, cans, and more. Mom picked up a green bottle.

"We will," said Mom. "That is the reason we came to the beach."

We gathered to hear a man speak.

He instructed us, "Pick up trash. But please leave shells, rocks, and seaweed. And keep on the beach! Do not get in the water now."

136

He told us to clean in teams. The three of us were a team. Each team got a trash bag.

137

MHEonline.com

Send all inquiries to:
McGraw-Hill Education
8787 Orion Place
Columbus, OH 43240

Be a Wrangler

by Martin Smith
illustrated by Karen Tafoya

Decodable Story 28

Bothell, WA • Chicago, IL • Columbus, OH • New York, NY

Knock! Knock! Knock! It is a fine April morning, saddle pals! Is it your first time here at the ranch?

You have a knack for this, partner! We can call you a wrangler now. And it is just the first morning on the ranch!

Get the knot on the rope just so. Hold your fingers, swing that arm, and twist that wrist. Toss and pull on the rope.

Are you glad we are here together, partner? We hope you have the best time! Write home to tell your pals all about it.

We offer horse rides here. A ranch visit is not complete until you get on a horse! Find a horse at the corral, partner.

Wranglers ride, and wranglers rope. You want a rope lesson, partner? Look at the wranglers with the ropes.

Step down off the horse, partner. We can brush and clean Sweet Pea. Then she can get a bite to eat.

These are the wranglers. Wranglers ride, and wranglers rope. The wranglers will assign you a horse to ride.

Here is the finest horse in these parts. Her name is Sweet Pea. She has a knack for being kind to humans.

That was a fine ride! You and Sweet Pea look cute together. Can we get a snapshot?

Is the ranch like you hoped it would be? Look out for those trees, partner! Wrap the rope around your hands. Ride on!

It's time to get on the horse. The wranglers will help. They know the ropes. Step on the cube to start!

Check that the knot is set. Step up here and pull on the saddle horn. Swing that leg over and settle in the saddle.

Ride on, partner! We will ride together with the wranglers. The wranglers go first, and we go behind. We will not go faster than the wranglers.

MHEonline.com

Send all inquiries to:
McGraw-Hill Education
8787 Orion Place
Columbus, OH 43240

Hit the Trail

by Susan Martina
illustrated by Barbara Counseller

Decodable Story 29

Bothell, WA • Chicago, IL • Columbus, OH • New York, NY

It may be a good day for a hike! Here are fun ways to hit the trail. First, let's read tips for safe hiking on the trail.

For example, you may find animals with a tail. Or, you may find things that are gray. You may make a list of them to remember the hike.

Alike Hike

Trail Tips

Look for things that are the same in some way. Pick one thing for the day.

14

Stay on the trail. It is the best way to be safe. And that way, you do not harm things in the wild.

3

Stay with your pals! There may be times when you want to hold hands and make a chain.

4

ANT!

Then find a thing that starts with the letter B and say its name. Keep playing until you get to Z.

13

A to Z Hike

To play, look for a thing that starts with the letter A. Say the name of the thing.

Take away those things that you bring. But let plants and animals stay right where they are.

Heads or Tails Hike

Can't agree which way to go? The heads or tails hike is best if you like to explore.

Or, you may take clay with you. Then you can make the shape of a plant you see on the trail.

Later you may make a painting from your sketch. If you have paints in a tray, you may take these on the trail.

Get a nickel and hike until you get to a spot where two trails cross. Flip the nickel.

If the nickel lands on heads, then take a right. If it lands on tails, take a left.

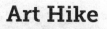

Art Hike

Take paper and pens with you on the trail. Make a quick sketch when stopping to rest.

MHEonline.com

Send all inquiries to:
McGraw-Hill Education
8787 Orion Place
Columbus, OH 43240

Granddaddy Spider

**an African tale
retold by Gordon Thomas
illustrated by Rachel Ivanyi**

Decodable Story 30

Bothell, WA • Chicago, IL • Columbus, OH • New York, NY

Now, spiders have little waists. But it was not this way long ago. Here is the story of how that happened.

By then, Granddaddy Spider's waist was tiny. And it remains that way to this day!

The tiny spiders tugged and tugged. Granddaddy was being squeezed by all the lines. Finally, the lines snapped.

One sunny day, Granddaddy Spider studied the bees as they gathered golden, sticky dust from a daisy.

"What will you do with all that dust?" asked nosey Granddaddy.

"Carry it back to the hive," buzzed the bees. "We need lots for the party."

Chimpanzee's and Zebra's parties started, too. Here came a third tug and then another.

In three days, Donkey's party started. A tiny spider tugged on the line. Just then Elephant's party started, and there was another tug.

"A party? That's funny," said Granddaddy. "I didn't hear of any party."

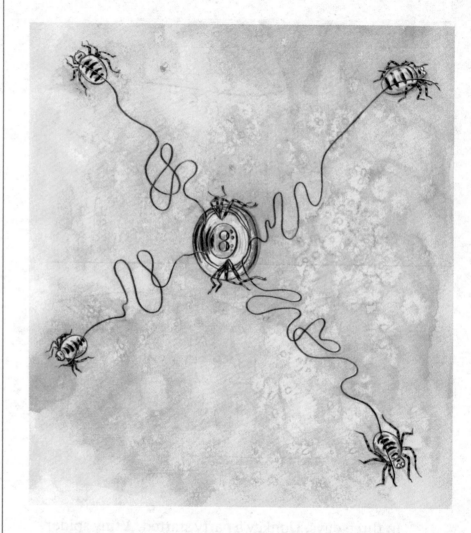

Granddaddy Spider went home. He drummed on his web to contact his grandkids. They were in each corner of the jungle. "Come home quickly!" he demanded.

He gave each tiny spider a line. "Carry these with you to your corner. When a party starts, tug on the line. Then I will know where to go."

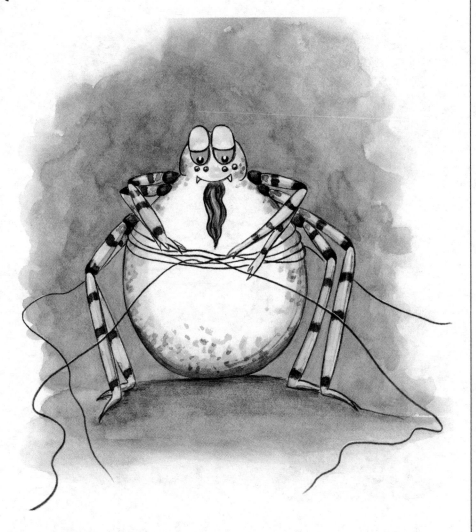

Granddaddy needed to know when a party started. He made a plan. He spun four long, silky lines. He wrapped each line around his middle.

The tiny spiders scurried home. "What is it, Granddaddy?" they asked.

"Who is going to have a party?" Granddaddy asked.

"It is Donkey," said a tiny spider.
"It is Elephant," said another.
"It is Chimpanzee," said a third.
"It is Zebra," said the last.

"I cannot believe it!" Granddaddy said. "Four parties? And each is in another corner of the jungle? How funny! But when?"

No one had any idea.

MHEonline.com

Send all inquiries to:
McGraw-Hill Education
8787 Orion Place
Columbus, OH 43240

Just a Phase
for Phil

by Martin Smith
illustrated by Barbara Counseller

Decodable Story 32

Bothell, WA • Chicago, IL • Columbus, OH • New York, NY

Phil had a wreck in here. To get on his bed, Phil had to climb over piles.

"Let me use this comb first," said Phil.
"This is a better phase, Phil," said his mom.

Tim knocked and came in.

"It looks so good in here! There is even a fresh scent." he said. "Let's take a photo!"

There were piles of wrinkled shirts, shorts, and pants. There were piles of belts with knots in them. There were piles of wrappers and paper.

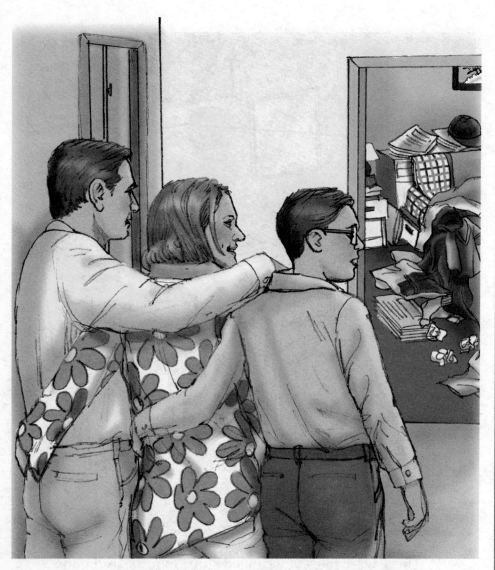

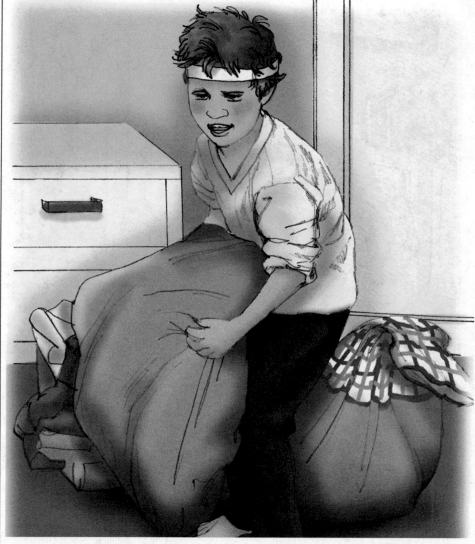

Phil's mom did not mind the wreck. "People can have a mess for a short time. This is just a phase for Phil," she said.

Phil built a big pile. He picked up the wrinkled shirts, shorts, and pants. Phil undid the knots in the belts. Phil picked up the wrappers and papers.

"What is this letter?" Phil asked. "Did a rock star write to me? Is this a scene from a play?"

Phil liked his wreck. He felt he had a knack for making a mess.

Phil liked to win, too. He had a knack for winning! Phil and Tim wanted to have a contest.

54

"Here is a wrench!" said Phil.
"Did a plumber forget it?" asked Tim.
"I don't know," answered Phil. "Here is a phone and a stuffed lamb!"

But Phil lost, so he had to listen to Tim and pick up the piles. What would people think of his character if he didn't?

They grabbed hands and gripped hard. Their knuckles hurt. Their thumbs went numb.

Then Phil's wrist hit the desk. Phil lost.
"Listen up, Phil. You must do what I tell you," said Tim.

56

"You must pick up the piles in here," said Tim.
"Humph!" said Phil as he began to wring his hands. He did not like this one bit.

57

MHEonline.com

Send all inquiries to:
McGraw-Hill Education
8787 Orion Place
Columbus, OH 43240

Meet the Firefighters

by Lynn Frankel
illustrated by Mary Kurnik Maass

Decodable Story 35

Bothell, WA • Chicago, IL • Columbus, OH • New York, NY

Hi! I'm Mike. Do you know what my job is? That's right! I'm a firefighter. I fight fires and answer cries for help.

98

Well, time to head back. It was my delight to meet you! And remember, check your fire alarms! It just might save a life!

III

That's what you need to do, too. If you are ever in a fire, stay down and get out fast. Do not cry and hide! It's wise to keep a flashlight near the bed.

This is where I work. It's open all the time. Fires can happen at any time, so we firefighters work day and night.

This is our fire truck. Like most fire trucks, it's red. We scrub and wax it a lot. We like it clean and bright.

There are times we must go in. Smoke rises, so we stay down. Smoke is dark. We use our lights. We get out as fast as we can.

There are times we need to get up high to fight a fire. Then we use ladders. This ladder can reach higher than 100 feet!

If there is a fire, this alarm bell rings. There are times when I'm asleep, and the bell rings. What a fright!

All the lights go on, and all the firefighters run. Some run down the flight of steps. I like to slide down the pole.

Some firefighters get the hose ready. Then they turn on the water. It comes out quite strongly.

We arrive at the fire site. First, we ask, "Is anyone in there?" We are lucky. No one is inside.

We get into the fire truck. Five firefighters ride this night. Let me tell you, it's pretty tight in here!

This fire truck needs two drivers. One drives in the regular spot, and one drives in the back.

We drive as fast as we can. The siren screams. The lights flash. This tells drivers, "Get out of our way!"

MHEonline.com

Copyright © 2015 McGraw-Hill Education

Send all inquiries to:
McGraw-Hill Education
8787 Orion Place
Columbus, OH 43240

A Green Leaf Print

by Martin Smith
illustrated by Dave Fischer

Decodable Story 37

Bothell, WA • Chicago, IL • Columbus, OH • New York, NY

What is the main difference between plants and animals? Think about this. Can an animal's body make a meal for itself?

What other things can you do with your leaf print? That is a challenge for you!

Make a spiral pad look fancy. Paste the print on the top. On the pages, sketch and write about trees! Write notes in the margins. Add some photos.

Well, green plants can feed themselves. Each plant is a little factory. Plants use the sun's rays to make a sweet substance. With that, plants can feed themselves.

You can see a thin slice of a green leaf under a microscope. That would reveal cells, or tiny parts, of the leaf.

Now what will you decide to do with a leaf print? You might make the print into a nice hanging. Simply paste the print to a stick and tie twine to it.

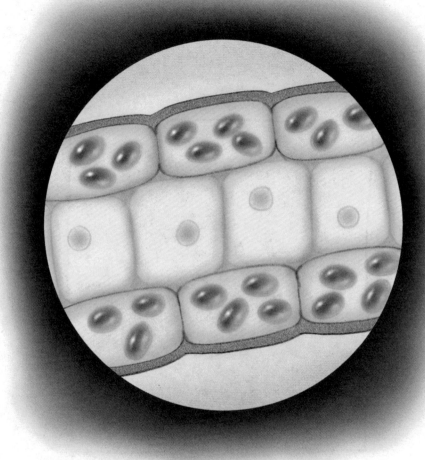

When you are done beating the leaf, lift up the fabric. Your print is complete. You will see the leaf's likeness in green. See how easy that was to make?

Several cells look like green jellybeans! These cells are the ones that get the job done.

Would you like to make a green leaf print? It is fun and easy to do.

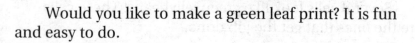

134

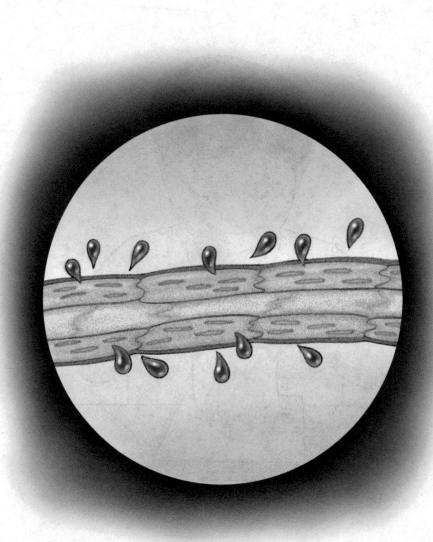

As you beat the leaf, the cells inside it are broken. This releases the green substance.

Use a rock to gently beat the fabric. Use even force. Trace around the edge of the leaf. Then beat the center.

Objects Needed to Make a Green Leaf Print
- green leaf
- piece of cotton fabric
- block
- thumbtacks
- rock

How to Make a Green Leaf Print

Start by picking a leaf from a tree limb. Try to pick a wide, flat leaf. Then lay the leaf on a block.

Align a piece of fabric on top of the leaf. Use thumbtacks to fasten the fabric in place.

MHEonline.com

Copyright © 2015 McGraw-Hill Education

Send all inquiries to:
McGraw-Hill Education
8787 Orion Place
Columbus, OH 43240

The Kitten's Rescue

by Edward Bricker
illustrated by Mary Kurnick Maass

Decodable Story 40

Bothell, WA • Chicago, IL • Columbus, OH • New York, NY

From my window I see Mrs. Fuse gazing up an oak tree. She is using a pole to poke the branches.

34

"Thank you for rescuing Hugo!" cries Mrs. Fuse.

"Don't thank us," replies Chief Logan. "Thank this smart fellow for calling us. He helped rescue Hugo. Sam is the real hero today!"

47

A firefighter named Joan uses a ladder to climb the tree and rescue Hugo.

"Hugo!" exclaims Mrs. Fuse. "You gave us quite a fright today!"

46

"Are you okay, Mrs. Fuse?" I ask.

"No!" she cries. "My kitten, Hugo, is stuck in the tree!"

35

"Hugo likes to see from the tree. But the tree is quite high, and he is afraid. Do you have a ladder we can use to rescue Hugo?" asks Mrs. Fuse.

36

Hugo starts to mew and does not stop.
"I think he's scared!" cries Mrs. Fuse.
"Our goal is to rescue Hugo as fast as we can," replies Chief Logan.

45

"Can you show us where the kitten is?" asks Chief Logan.

"Hugo is sitting on that huge branch at the top of that oak tree. I know he wants to get down!" cries Mrs. Fuse.

44

"No, I don't," I tell Mrs. Fuse. "But I will call Fire Chief Logan. He will rescue Hugo."

"Thank you, Sam!" cries Mrs. Fuse.

37

"Mrs. Fuse's cat, Hugo, is stuck in a tree!" I tell Mom. "I need to help rescue him."

38

When the red truck stops, a few firefighters jump off the back. Fire Chief Logan runs over to Mrs. Fuse and me.

43

We see a huge, red fire truck down the road. A few moments later, it gets to my home.

"Use this," Mom replies, as she hands me her phone. I make the call, and a nice lady responds, "Fire and Rescue, how may I help you?"

"Yes," I say. "A cute little kitten named Hugo is trapped in a tree. I am hoping Fire Chief Logan could come rescue him."

"My name is Sam Smith. I live at 35 Cuba Lane."
"I will send the fire truck right away," the lady replies.

MHEonline.com

Send all inquiries to:
McGraw-Hill Education
8787 Orion Place
Columbus, OH 43240

A Plant that Acts Like an Animal

by Elizabeth Ramsey
illustrated by Dave Fischer

Decodable Story 46

Bothell, WA • Chicago, IL • Columbus, OH • New York, NY

Like animals, plants adapt to their surroundings. One such plant is the Venus flytrap. It grows in bogs and marshes. Its roots cannot get the food it needs from the marsh. So the Venus flytrap eats bugs. This plant truly acts like an animal!

The Venus flytrap eats flies, crickets, spiders, slugs, and more. It does not have a mouth, but it still gets full. The pictures on the next two pages show how a plant can eat.

In the past, a lot of Venus flytraps grew in the wild. Now, few are left there. Over the years, people took many of them home.

Some marshes and bogs are dirty. Some have been cleared for human use. For these reasons, wild flytraps are endangered. Now it's a rule that people can no longer dig them up.

However, you can get a Venus flytrap at a plant store. Look over these tips on how to raise your own Venus flytrap.

- Plant flytrap in a mix of peat moss and sand.
- Add water to keep dirt wet.
- Don't forget to feed your flytrap!

- Leaves form a trap.
- Sweet, sticky sap attracts an insect.

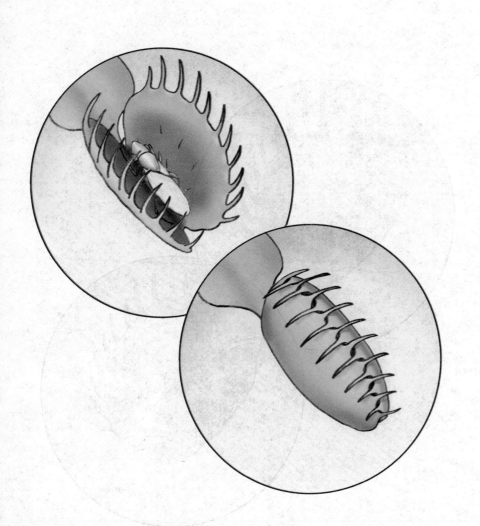

What happens if you put your finger in the trap? It will not pounce on your finger. The trap will close part of the way and then open again. It can tell which things are good to eat!

The Venus flytrap cannot chow down on large insects. The trap must be able to close and make an airtight pouch. If the trap does not close all the way, mold and other bad things will enter the trap. The trap may turn brown and drop to the ground. Then the plant will make a new trap.

When the trap closes, however, it's chow time! Picture this: Acid seeps into the trap. This acid lets the plant digest the bug. It may take a week or more. Then the trap opens.

- The leaves snap shut and hook together.
- The insect is stuck, and the plant begins the process.

MHEonline.com

Send all inquiries to:
McGraw-Hill Education
8787 Orion Place
Columbus, OH 43240

How Roy Got a Toy Drum

by Elizabeth Ramsey
illustrated by Valeria Cis

Decodable Story 48

Bothell, WA • Chicago, IL • Columbus, OH • New York, NY

Next Roy met the baker. He had no bread to sell.

"I have flour but no oil," he said.

"Without oil, I cannot make bread."

Roy gave him the oil. The baker held out a sheet of shiny foil.

"Do you want this?"

"Yes, please!" said Roy.

Roy shaped the foil into a glittering toy. Soon an old man came along.

"I want that toy for my granddaughter," he said.

"Will you accept this coin for it?"

Roy raced to the store. He pointed at the toy drum and showed the seller his coin. At last, the toy drum was his! With joy, Roy joined a band.

Roy was a boy who lived with his mom. Roy really wanted to have a toy drum. Roy's mom worked hard in the soil to grow food. She could not afford a toy drum for Roy.

Roy's mom wanted to get Roy the toy drum. But she didn't have a single coin.

Walking home, she found a coil of rope.

"It's not much," she thought, "but I'll give this to Roy."

Roy thanked his mom for the coil of rope.

"Thanks. It's nice of you to think of me," Roy said.

Soon he met the potter, who was yelling at his goat.

"What's wrong?" asked Roy.

"I need a rope to tie this goat. She always runs off."

Roy gave the potter his coil of rope. The happy potter gave Roy a pot.

Next Roy met a lady with children. The crying children were making an awful noise.

"What's wrong?" asked Roy.

"They are hungry," the lady said.

"I have rice but no pot to boil it in."

Roy gave her his pot.

"Take this oil," the lady said.

"I have too much, and it will spoil."

MHEonline.com

Copyright © 2015 McGraw-Hill Education

Send all inquiries to:
McGraw-Hill Education
8787 Orion Place
Columbus, OH 43240

Brave After All

by Margaret Mason
illustrated by Valeria Cis

Decodable Story 49

Bothell, WA • Chicago, IL • Columbus, OH • New York, NY

Then one day, Paul's hound got loose. All the animals ran. But the turtle could not crawl fast.

Soon Paul's hound had the turtle in his jaws. The turtle shook from fear.

Scout and Joy ran to help.

"Silly hound, put that turtle down on the ground," Joy said calmly.

"Turtles are not good to eat. That shell will give your tummy an awful pain."

Paul's hound thought a bit and frowned. Then he dropped the turtle and trotted away.

The turtle told all the animals how brave the cats were. Now, all the animals were in awe of Scout and Joy. They felt bad for teasing the brave cats.

"Both of you are brave after all," the turtle said.

One fall day, a boy and a girl found a pair of fine-looking cats. They made a choice to adopt the cats and took them home at once. They called the cats Scout and Joy. They taught Scout and Joy all about their new house.

"Just look out for Paul's big hound!" the boy said.

Scout and Joy were small white cats. They were both pretty and sweet. And they always stayed together.

They liked to stalk bugs on the lawn and clown around with a ball of yarn. The boy once gave them a foil ball for a toy. The girl gave them moist cat food. Scout and Joy enjoyed their nice, easy life.

Soon all the animals began to tease Scout and Joy. They thought the cats were spoiled.

There was a bird who would laugh at them for always staying together.

"They're afraid," cackled the bird. "Look how they cling together! Those small cats are even afraid of loud noises!"

Scout and Joy ignored the animals because they knew it wasn't true.

"I hope they never meet Paul's big hound!" teased the turtle. "They'll wish they could crawl into a shell!"

All the animals laughed.

"Pretty kitties, do you even have claws?"

Scout and Joy were not annoyed. They had no cause to let fools upset them.

MHEonline.com

Send all inquiries to:
McGraw-Hill Education
8787 Orion Place
Columbus, OH 43240

Little Havana in Miami

by Grace Trubiano
illustrated by Robert Casilla

Decodable Story 50

Bothell, WA • Chicago, IL • Columbus, OH • New York, NY

You know that people from different places came to live in America. What did they bring with them? Although it was a tough choice, they brought things that made them feel at home.

Different communities have different ways of doing things. Foods, music, art, and ways of talking and celebrating are part of the way of life in a community.

The community often has street parties. There is food, Latin music, Cuban dance, and street theater. The community has a big festival each year in March. It is thought to be one of the biggest festivals in the United States. You will see people of all ages. They will be singing, dancing, and eating in the Cuban way!

A well-known place in Little Havana is Domino Park. It has enough tables and chairs for a lot of people to play dominoes. This was a game people played in Havana, Cuba, and then they brought it with them to America.

Tower Art Center is another place in Little Havana that lets you know about the way of life here. You can see Spanish films, singers, dancers, and such at the Tower Art Center. Local artists display their paintings in nearby galleries.

So what kinds of foods, music, art, and ways of talking and celebrating are found in Little Havana? This part of Miami, Florida, is all about Cuba.

Cubans have been living south Florida since the early 1900s. But in the 1960s, large numbers of Cubans began leaving their homes. Many sought a new life in Little Havana.

Part of Miami is known as Little Havana. As soon as you step into Little Havana, you get the flavor of Cuba. You might hear Spanish music. As you walk around the streets, you will find delights enjoyed by those who live there.

You will see places that offer Cuban foods. People here might try a beef dish or real coconut. There are also pork and chicken sandwiches. They look so good, you ought to ask the clerk to wrap up a few! There are also many stores that sell all kinds of goods from Spain and Latin America.

MHEonline.com

Little India in Chicago

by Dennis Fertig
illustrated by Luanne Marten

Decodable Story 51

Bothell, WA • Chicago, IL • Columbus, OH • New York, NY

Big cities like Chicago are filled with people from many different places. Often these people build communities within the city.

People from South Asia began to arrive in the United States in the 1970s. They came from India, Pakistan, and Bangladesh. In Chicago, many of these people settled in an area around Devon Avenue. Today, that area is often called Little India.

Some of the buildings around Devon Avenue have South Asian designs. These designs may include pointed arches or bright reds and yellows. Some places teach South Asian kids and adults to read, write, and speak English.

Some city street signs on Devon Avenue show names of well-known people in the history of India, Pakistan, and Bangladesh. Other signs show names of well-known people from other far-off lands. That is because Devon Avenue is like Chicago and the United States. It is home to people from all over the planet.

A summer highlight is the India Day parade down Devon Avenue. Families line up on the street to see floats, dancers, bands, and singers. Kids climb high on tree limbs to enjoy all the excitement. Visitors take photo after photo!

South Asian people changed the look and feel of Devon Avenue. Walking down the street is a treat. It is often crowded with people from the community as well as visitors. Some visitors are South Asian people from around Chicago or from other parts of the United States.

All enjoy a delightful scene. Rich smells of curry, such as cloves, bay leaves, nutmeg, and cinnamon fill visitors' noses. Signs on shops tell of sales on films, cell phones, books, and much more.

Food markets have open stands on the sidewalks. Next to them, other shops display racks of bright South Asian clothing. Inside, shoppers find scented soaps, bracelets, and wristbands. Or they find pretty combs, knit scarves, and rings for fingers and thumbs!

Many visitors come to Little India to eat. The street has both simple snack shops and fancy dining places. A common treat is a kabob, which is spicy meat grilled on a stick. Lamb and chicken kabobs are favorites.

Little Italy in New York

by Susan Martin
illustrated by Lyle Miller

Decodable Story 52

Bothell, WA • Chicago, IL • Columbus, OH • New York, NY

Think about going to live in a new land. It will take much strength to make such a long trip. When you get to the United States, everything is new and strange. You ache for the feeling of home. You ought to make this new place feel like home. What can you do?

Say that you know people who also came to America from your old home. Will you spread out all over the new city? Or will you try to stay in the same place?

All around Little Italy, signs use red, white, and green. Why? This is just like the flag of Italy!

There are many places to eat that offer tastes from Italy. Most people think the food is splendid! Along these streets, different shops sell foods and goods made in Italy.

Each autumn, this community has a big festival. It celebrates a person who meant a lot to the people of Italy, particularly those from Naples, Italy. This festival lasts over 11 days! People gather to see parades, listen to music, and eat good food. They thoroughly celebrate both Italy and life in America!

You thought it might be easier to stay together. It is rough to learn everything about the new land on your own. Then more and more people head out for America and find you in your new place.

When enough people gather together, you build a new community. Then you try to create scenes and scents that feel a bit like your old home. Which sights and smells remind you of the place you grew up?

How is Little Italy in New York City like home for people who came from Italy? Just stroll along the streets to find the answer!

In the late 1800s, many people came to New York from Italy. At that time, life in Italy was tough with very few jobs. So many came to New York to start a new life.

In America, people from Italy found new jobs. They opened shops and places to eat. They all lived in the same place. This place became known as Little Italy.

Places change over time. Although Little Italy does not sprawl over as many city blocks as it once did, the ties to Italy still remain strong.

MHEonline.com

Chinatown in San Francisco

by Gordon Thomas
illustrated by Jane McCreary

Decodable Story 53

Bothell, WA • Chicago, IL • Columbus, OH • New York, NY

Many people came to the United States from different lands. They came in search of a better life, and they settled in major cities. They based their new lives on the ways they knew from back home. In time, entire areas took on the feel of the old land.

Let's take a look at one of these communities. Let's learn a little more about Chinatown in San Francisco. You can find something new around each corner of this community.

The party ends with a big parade. It is filled with floats and people in costume. There are bands and dancers, too. The last thing in the parade is a huge dragon that seems to dance slowly down the street. It's a time of hope for a bright New Year.

Chinatown is a community full of life. It is filled with shops, good food, art galleries, and museums. Many people visit it because it gives such an interesting look at the Chinese ways of doing things. And many people know Chinatown as their home.

People in Chinatown get in a festive mood for the Chinese New Year. They show respect to the older people in their families. Children get red envelopes with new dollar bills. Firecrackers are set off to greet the New Year.

Chinatown has a long history. In the 1800s, many laborers came to San Francisco from China. Now the community is a mix of old and new. It's also true that Chinatown hosts many visitors each year.

Enter Chinatown at the Dragon's Gate. Then you have your first clue that you are in a Chinese community. You can walk down narrow streets jammed with rows of shops. Inside, you can buy things usually found in shops in China. There are foods, toys, flowers in bloom, and much more. Crowds of people fill every nook of the market.

The best food shopping is at a market on Saturday afternoons. Sellers offer produce they have grown. They also sell live animals such as turtles, chickens, and more. These markets get very crowded.

Speaking of food, Chinatown offers lots of good places to eat. There are family noodle bars and fancy places to eat. Many give a true taste of China.

MHEonline.com

Send all inquiries to:
McGraw-Hill Education
8787 Orion Place
Columbus, OH 43240

Polish Communities in Detroit

by Martin Smith
illustrated by Leslie Brown

Decodable Story 54

Bothell, WA • Chicago, IL • Columbus, OH • New York, NY

What have you found out about people who come to live in the United States? Here are some clues. They often bring foods, music, and ways of talking and celebrating with them.

People often feel proud of their roots. When they go to live in a new place, they keep some old ways of doing things.

Which roots are people in Hamtramck proud about? Most people in this city have Polish roots. This community is near downtown Detroit. In fact, Detroit surrounds the city on all sides. Hamtramck is a city within a city.

One way of celebrating Polish roots is with a Polish wedding. These weddings can last all day. After the wedding in a church, the bride and groom have a party in a big hall. A band plays with a singer, drums, a trumpet, and even a tuba. People dance to the loud music. They might dance something called the Polish Hop or the waltz. People also enjoy all the best Polish foods and drinks.

It would be nice if you saw a Polish wedding, but there are all kinds of ways to enjoy customs from Poland. There are many places in these communities to eat Polish foods, hear music, and go dancing!

People came to America from Poland in the early 1900s. It is hard to say just how many people from Poland came to America. But now, many people with Polish roots can be found near Detroit because some people first came to work in the auto plants near the city.

The communities changed over time, but the Polish roots stayed in place. Even now, you can hear the sounds of people talking Polish in communities. Places that serve Polish food draw a lot of people. So do places where Polish music and dancing are found.

If you go to visit this city, then count on trying some Polish foods. Eat the tasty stew with meats and mushrooms. Try the cucumber salad or the Polish sandwich with veggies baked inside. Many people count dumplings served with sour cream to be a real treat.

Also near Detroit is another community with Polish roots. Orchard Lake is home to the Polish-American Sports Hall of Fame. This museum pays tribute to outstanding Polish-American athletes in baseball, softball, football, basketball, and a few more sports.

MHEonline.com

Send all inquiries to:
McGraw-Hill Education
8787 Orion Place
Columbus, OH 43240

The Seminole Tribe in South Florida

by Gordon Thomas
illustrated by Robert Casilla

Decodable Story 55

Bothell, WA • Chicago, IL • Columbus, OH • New York, NY

Would you like to hear a Seminole legend? Late at night, Seminole children used to listen to the elders, or older people, telling stories. Stories about the past are still important to the Seminole people. Storytellers must do their best to retell a story well, without changing any details.

The past is very important to the Seminole Tribe. Although, so is the present day, and all those days yet to come!

There are more than enough places to shop on the Seminole lands. Shirts, skirts, and other items have Seminole designs. Artists make baskets and beadwork.

You can try Seminole foods, too, like fry bread or even alligator meat.

You can also book a boat ride into the wetlands. You may see raccoons, water buffalo, wild hogs, hawks, alligators, or even panthers! Later, you might be surprised to see a Seminole wrestle an alligator in a show!

You know that people came from many places to live in America. You also are likely to know that America had people living here long before any settlers came.

There were a large number of communities of Native Americans living throughout what is now the United States. Let's look at the Seminole Tribe found in south Florida.

History experts say that the Seminole Tribe can be traced back at least 12,000 years. The Seminoles' life was based on the land. They caught fish and hunted animals.

Settlers from Spain first came to that land about 500 years ago. More folks came and wanted to live on the land, too. Over time, life began to change for the Seminoles.

Now the Seminole Tribe owns much land in south Florida. You can visit these lands to learn more about Seminole life. You can learn about Seminole life in the past and now.

You ought to visit a museum. The museum tells how the Seminole people lived in the Florida wetlands. A film shows the Seminoles' history as well as the struggles they faced when settlers wanted them to leave their land.

You can see a chickee hut. These were built by the Seminole people long ago as a kind of house. Really, chickees were more like a tent. The Seminole people used them for only a short time. Chickees are dry palm leaves over a log frame. These shelters could be made quickly and also left quickly, if necessary.

Decodable Stories Table

Getting Started

Lesson	Core Decodable	Practice Decodable	Sound/Spelling Correspondences	High-Frequency Words Introduced
Day 2	1 Sand, Tan Hats, and a Mat	1 Nat's Hats	/s/ spelled *s, ss* /m/ spelled *m* /t/ spelled *t, tt* /d/ spelled *d* /n/ spelled *n* /h/ spelled *h_* /a/ spelled *a*	give may these
Day 3	2 Hats!	2 Ants! Ants! Ants!	Review Day 2	
Day 4	3 Cass, Bill, and Mitt	3 Milt and Tam, a Tan Cat	/l/ spelled *l, ll* /b/ spelled *b* /k/ spelled *c* /i/ spelled *i*	
Day 5	4 Mitts and Hits	4 Ants at a Lamp	/k/ spelled *k* /p/ spelled *p* /r/ spelled *r* Review /i/	been our those
Day 6	5 A Big Fan	5 Grant Ran!	/f/ spelled *f, ff* /g/ spelled *g* /o/ spelled *o*	off
Day 7	6 A Best Pig Pin	6 Lists!	/j/ spelled *j* /ks/ spelled *x* /w/ spelled *w_* /e/ spelled *e, _ea_*	Mr. Mrs. read
Day 8	7 A Contest	7 Jeff and Max	Review /o/ /e/	stop tell who
Day 9	8 Gwen Must Run	8 Val's Van	/kw/ spelled *qu_* /v/ spelled *v* /y/ spelled *y_* /z/ spelled *z, zz, _s* /u/ spelled *u*	ten us
Day 10	9 Buzz, Buzz, Buzz	9 Gram's Land	Review consonants and short vowel sounds and spellings	

Unit 1

Lesson	Core Decodable	Practice Decodable	Sound/Spelling Correspondences	High-Frequency Words Introduced
Lesson 1	10 Chips	10 Finch Ranch	/ch/ spelled *ch* /th/ spelled *th* /sh/ spelled *sh*	far upon
	11 The Red Star	11 Bart's Farm Trip	/w/ spelled *wh_* /ar/ spelled *ar*	much start which
Lesson 2	12 A Bridge	12 Pudge Runs	/j/ spelled *dge* /k/ spelled *ck* /ch/ spelled *tch*	never under
Lesson 3	13 A Lunch List	13 Fluff	Review Unit 1 Lessons 1–2 Inflectional endings *-s, -es, -ed*	eight nine
Lesson 4	14 No Drinks in Class	14 Chuck's Shack	/ng/ spelled *ng* /nk/ spelled *nk* Inflectional ending *-ing*	bring thank think
	15 Paddle, Duck, Paddle	15 A Pink Gift	Schwa /əl/ spelled *el, le, al, il*	seven use why
Lesson 5	16 Learning to Swim	16 Pearl Helps Burt	/er/ spelled *er, ir, ur, ear*	better first learn
	17 Farm Chores	17 Mort on His Porch	/or/ spelled *or, ore*	animal black horse
Lesson 6	18 Tracks at a Pond	18 Turtle Shop	Review Unit 1	live

Unit 2

Lesson	Core Decodable	Practice Decodable	Sound/Spelling Correspondences	High-Frequency Words Introduced
Lesson 1	19 Kate's Picnic	19 A Fake Snake	/ā/ spelled *a, a_e*	brother
	20 Five Gifts for Mike	20 Iris's Kite	/ī/ spelled *i, i_e*	white
Lesson 2	21 The Mole Zone	21 A Surprise for Hope	/ō/ spelled *o, o_e*	both hold open
	22 Hope's Cute Music Box	22 Nick's Bugle Music	/ū/ spelled *u, u_e*	buy goes paste zero
Lesson 3	23 A Good Life at the Lake	23 Backyard Life	Review Unit 2 Lessons 1–2 Comparative ending *-er* and superlative ending *-est*	another many
	24 Uncle Jack	24 April's Grade	/n/ spelled *kn_, gn* /r/ spelled *wr_*	sign uncle write
Lesson 4	25 Edith and Pete	25 Hints	/ē/ spelled *e, e_e*	because does
	26 Amazing Animals	26 Rose Rides	Review all long vowels	often other horse taste
Lesson 5	27 A Good Deed at the Beach	27 A Hike East	Review /ē/ spelled *e, e_e, ee, ea*	please three
Lesson 6	28 Be a Wrangler	28 Diving for Shipwrecks	Review Unit 2	pull together

Unit 3

Lesson	Core Decodable	Practice Decodable	Sound/Spelling Correspondences	High-Frequency Words Introduced
Lesson 1	29 Hit the Trail	29 Sailing in Rain	Review /ā/ spelled *a, a_e, ai_, _ay*	gray
Lesson 2	30 Granddaddy Spider	30 Missy's Next Story	Review /ē/ spellings	believe carry
Lesson 3	31 Meet the Bats	31 Cleaning for Gramps	Review Unit 3 Lessons 1–2	different only
	32 Just a Phase for Phil	32 Mom's Chore Chart	/f/ spelled *ph* /m/ spelled *_mb* Silent letters	listen people
Lesson 4	33 A Force in the Dirt	33 A Trip?	/s/ spelled *ce, ci_, cy*	again center circle
	34 Uncle Gene	34 Ginger the General	/j/ spelled *ge, gi_*	great
Lesson 5	35 Meet the Firefighters	35 Nightlights	/ī/ spelled *_igh, _ie, _y*	light work
	36 Try My Pie	36 A Nice Race	Review /ī/ spellings	myself
Lesson 6	37 A Green Leaf Print	37 A Deal	Review Unit 3	done easy piece

Unit 4

Lesson	Core Decodable	Practice Decodable	Sound/Spelling Correspondences	High-Frequency Words Introduced
Lesson 1	38 The Boat Show	38 A Load of Apples	/ō/ spelled _ow, oa_, o, o_e	own show
Lesson 2	39 A Stroll on Mule Street	39 The Museum	/ū/ spelled _ew, _ue, u, u_e	few
Lesson 3	40 The Kitten's Rescue	40 A Hot Band	Review Unit 4 Lessons 1–2	today quite
Lesson 4	41 Under the Moon	41 Scooter and the Goose	/ōō/ spelled oo	soon
Lesson 5	42 Drew's True Lesson	42 A Robin's Red Plumes	/ōō/ spelled u, u_e, _ew, _ue	knew new something sorry
Lesson 6	43 Sue, Joan, and Mud	43 Ruby's Band	Review Unit 4	everyone

Unit 5

Lesson	Core Decodable	Practice Decodable	Sound/Spelling Correspondences	High-Frequency Words Introduced
Lesson 1	44 Look How Pets Adapt	44 The Rookie Firefighter	/oo/ spelled oo	warm wash
Lesson 2	45 Mr. Brown Sees the World	45 Max Brown Strikes Out	/ow/ spelled ow, ou_	
Lesson 3	46 A Plant that Acts Like an Animal	46 Animal Expert in Outer Space	Review Unit 5 Lessons 1–2	full picture
Lesson 4	47 The Lion and the Mouse	47 The Bootmaker's Daughter	/aw/ spelled aw, au_, augh, ough, all, al	mouse ought small
Lesson 5	48 How Roy Got a Toy Drum	48 The Koi at the Dragon Gate	/oi/ spelled oi, _oy	always
Lesson 6	49 Brave After All	49 A Talk with Gramps	Review Unit 5	laugh once

Unit 6

Lesson	Core Decodable	Practice Decodable	Sound/Spelling Correspondences	High-Frequency Words Introduced
Lesson 1	50 Little Havana in Miami	50 Nancy's Tryout	ough spelling pattern	brought
Lesson 2	51 Little India in Chicago	51 Island of the Gnome	Review silent letters	
Lesson 3	52 Little Italy in New York	52 Christopher's Diner	Review Unit 6 Lessons 1–2	everything
Lesson 4	53 Chinatown in San Francisco	53 The Music Fest	Contrast/ōō/ and /oo/, /ō/ and /ow/	
Lesson 5	54 Polish Communities in Detroit	54 A Drawing on the Wall	Contrast /ōō/ and /ū/, /aw/ and /ow/	
Lesson 6	55 The Seminole Tribe in South Florida	55 Communities in Los Angeles	Review Unit 6	

Grade 2 High-Frequency Words

again	easy	many	people	these
always	eight	may	picture	think
animal	everyone	mouse	piece	those
another	everything	Mr.	please	three
because	far	Mrs.	pull	today
been	few	much	quite	together
believe	first	myself	read	uncle
better	full	never	seven	under
black	give	new	show	upon
both	goes	nine	sign	us
bring	gray	off	small	use
brother	great	often	something	warm
brought	hold	once	soon	wash
buy	horse	only	sorry	which
carry	knew	open	start	white
center	laugh	other	stop	who
circle	learn	ought	taste	why
different	light	our	tell	work
does	listen	own	ten	write
done	live	paste	thank	zero

Grade 1 High-Frequency Words

about	come	how	one	too
after	could	if	or	two
an	day	into	over	very
any	don't	its	pretty	walk
are	every	jump	put	want
around	five	just	red	water
ask	four	know	ride	way
away	from	like	right	well
before	get	long	saw	went
big	going	make	six	where
blue	good	me	sleep	will
brown	got	my	take	would
by	green	no	their	yellow
call	help	now	them	yes
came	here	old	this	your

Grade K High-Frequency Words

a	did	her	on	they
all	do	him	out	to
am	down	his	said	up
and	for	I	see	was
as	girl	in	she	we
at	go	is	some	were
be	had	it	that	what
boy	has	little	the	when
but	have	look	then	with
can	he	of	there	you